Ink for an Odd Cartography

Black Lawrence Press

www.blacklawrence.com

Executive Editor and Art Director: Colleen Ryor
Managing Editor: Diane Goettel
Book Design: Steven Seighman and Colleen Ryor

Black Lawrence Press
8405 Bay Parkway C8
Brooklyn, N.Y. 11214
U.S.A.

Published 2009 by Black Lawrence Press, a division of Dzanc Books

First edition 2009

Printed in the United States

Ink for an Odd Cartography

poems

Michele Battiste

Black Lawrence Press
New York

Contents

Mapping the Spaces Between

Coda

Marking the Boundaries

My mind moves in more than one place,
In a country half-land, half-water.
— Theodore Roethke, "The Far Field"

Like a Sine Curve

So you know how the skin of whales
    not all whales but some whales
    maybe all whales
the skin of whales, the exoderm, if
    that's a word, but you see my emphasis
contains an intricate pattern of tiny muscles
    tiny like an eyelid muscle
    the muscle that may cause a tic
    and tic is the small movement I want you
    to envision
an intricate pattern of tiny muscles that move independently
    so maybe think of grass in wind
    each blade bending one nanosecond
    before the other
each whale skin muscle contracting before the other as the whale propels
itself through water
    so you may be thinking ripple
    but not as a fan unfolds, more
    like a sine curve, which you would think of,
    which naval researchers would think
    of when they think about improving
    the aerodynamical (or would it be
    aquadynamical) structure
    of their submarines, working the water
    like a whale works the water
without thinking, its skin a series of muscular shudders driving water
along its flank, quickening

So you know how whale skin can do that?
I do that
I do that sometimes but not swimming
I know what you're thinking: the misappropriation of sine curves, but
focus
I am not whale skin
I am the water that moves with the muscle
You are the whale

Climbing Brian

This is not a love poem, though photos may prove
    otherwise, not as an elm proves belligerence, but as a knot
    of eels proves fear – dark bodies of water
If bodies can be mountains then Brian is a swell without rockface,
    switchbacks overgrown with clover, trail markers faded
    to mere suggestion
Required gear: compass, cornstarch, savory victuals for bait,
    for slowing the ascent, for remembering the tongue
    is a strong muscle

Tape the bruised toe but no shoes
The back of his bent knees are footholds
Footholds yield to soft pressure
Not everyone can climb Brian
Little dancers who know how to fall often do

There is a center, a contempt of gravity, a plumb-line-determined
    nexus of nerves that would rather float than balance
Some swear by abdominals but the pelvis is better – light
    for the hollow
Raised, it will hover and billow, shadow his back
    not as a parachute shadows a fall, but as a storm
    cloud shadows, distended above dark bodies of water, and arms
    will forget there should be mass for the balancing
Strong muscles are good
Hands then knees then feet on shoulders
Higher than Brian is higher than a mountain, a body
All bodies are mostly water

No Swimming

We begin aquatic, gills barely formed
then gone before we breach surface, gasping
at that alien air. It's a blessing,
to scratch lightly at our necks, not knowing
a phantom respiration wants to drown,
to return to water and let the waves

resuscitate our throats and watch us wave
goodbye to bread and steak. It was a form
of wishing, when I, at three, almost drowned
in the neighbor's pool, yanked out and gasping,
kicking to stay under, somehow knowing
womb and death share the same sleep and blessing.

Panic also moonlights as a blessing
when we swim beyond the breakers, the waves
gravid and gently swelling. We know
a demon's beckoning takes many forms
and recognition sends us back, gasping
for shore, flailing, afraid not of drowning

but of our unfathomable urge to drown.
It isn't death we want, but rest, to bless
each limb with weightlessness, to gasp
at the loss of being's burden waving
in the current as it descends. Then form-
less in consciousness, our bodies knowing

nothing but suspension, we'd suspect nothing
exists for reasons other than to drown
out the world we were forced into. Forming
embryonic shapes in sleep like a blessed
infante with no realm claimed, no waving
to distant minions, a body grasps

its oceanic start — the final gasp
strikes the same cosmic chord as the first. "Know
this," the body says, waking, waving
its arms as if remembering a drowned
doppelganger, "these bones, this skin, a blessing
of breath and a nervous foot tap don't form

the end. I'm drowning in you, you're forming
into a wave of air gasped by some god
who knows to bless each beginning, but won't."

Commitment

This church drowns, legs
kicking and churning eddies
at the altar, the sacristy filmed
with silt. I am not to mourn
here, my shoes ruined
with stickseed and blister
juice, my sorrow like milk-
weed forced from its pod.

The plane plummets, the car
crashes, the millet rusts
across the road. This side,
windrows are thinning
and wait to be baled
and the babies are impatient
underground, smacking
their fists at roots. Soil
shrivels in the autumn drought.

The Reverend Myrtle Tuttle
predicted gravel and a foul
moon. My love, one day
I will marry you, bend
to pick up blossoms
that drop from my crown.
I promise I will lose
the map of the cemetery,
a penciled circle marking
your collapsed mound.

Mapping the Places

Beautiful my desire, and the place of my desire.

— Theodore Roethke, "The Rose"

Your Bed

was a caravan of gypsies without country –
rucksacks of clavicle, of salt-licked crimson,
slivers of silvered skin crossing palm,
a faded deck of tarot, fingertipped and risking
the upturned card of fool.

Every border crossing claimed a changeling,
    demon-blooded limbs
    that twitched with every touch
    of othered skin.
Was I the stolen child or were you?
We were too tangled to tell.

The gypsies passed and cast a tarantella to our bones.

In the morning they are searching for a homeland.
In the morning we trace their tracks like reading Braille,
    like telling fortunes,
    like the newly baptized wanting so much
    to believe.

Ruby Skye

I know how to handle my men.
Like vodka
    one slow sip after another with hardly a breath between.
Feel every burn, every cowed demon begging
    permission to get inside, to chance a possession.

This place is filled with fallen angels,
    calls them with a beacon of marquee neon that makes
    all of Mason Street ache for redemption.
Ruby Skye

    resurrecting those few exquisite moments before
    Gomorrah burned.
I've played Lot's wife for centuries and I'm sick of it.
Call me Lillith.
I know how to handle my men.

He could be taller,
    could speak more distinctly,
but he took my hand with a vestige of seraphim authority
    and I'll ache for him soon enough.

It's elegant, really.
The dancing girls in g-strings and bejeweled bras.
The granite-topped bars, mica flecks seizing candlelight to feed
    their own flicker.
The DJ more blacksmith than artist, smelting a frenzy in 4/4 beat,
    relentless and hammering.
The ice in every glass more ember than freeze.
A hundred bodies all in heat.
And from this mass he chose me.

There are travelers among us. Tourists.
Trifling with excess and flesh as if sin is some attraction
    they can scrapbook. Wake in the morning. Move on.

The denizens abandoned sin epochs ago, an adolescent fad
    compared to our affliction.
No brimstone can crush it, no 40-day flood can wash
    us clean.

This one's been around, but we descended differently.
He is fallen. I climbed three ladders down and touched
    a lit match to the wood.
Some say I've stashed a pair of stolen wings for a prodigal return
    to obedience.
Some say I intimidate the devil.
Yesterday I played air hockey for erotic favors instead of points
    and if that's one of nine circles I'm ready for another round
    and he hasn't heard the rumors.

Last call.
I name him Arakial and tease him for a drink.
Run my fingers along the blades that replaced wings
    and remind us each of the mistake no one can forgive.
Dancing girls trip like pigeons off the stage.
He wants my address, my name.
I tell him Lillith,
    wait for him to realize I've played him
    like a child's game.

He takes me by the hair and whispers,
    tongue forked, poison in my ear,
Darling, let me tell you what I did to get here.

Happy Immortal

1.   Patrick and I bought rings today.
Somewhere between the beer
garden and bandstand, a booth
at the street festival lured
dollars from our pockets
and now a moonstone webbed
in silver wraps around
my toe. Patrick slipped
it on, and I chose for him
a Celtic band of spirals and which hand,
which finger.

It was accidental, our wants coinciding,
lack not our only motivation.
And it was accidental, the way we lost
each other in the crowd as we moved on.

2.   Patrick says love is viral, an affliction nesting
in your blood after the infection, becoming
your biology, dying
only when you die. It erupts
when the body's weak, blistering
like herpes, and you wait
for the symptoms to fade, like they did
once, to every appearance of gone.

Patrick thinks he's speaking a metaphor,
but I know an ache and an itch
and a swelling and a fever when I feel
them coming on.

3.   In eight days the moon will cut
across the earth, eclipsing sun. It's not divine,
how celestial bodies line up sometimes,
the heavens asking for a little more
attention. Like bumping into your ex-lover
at the Thai food stand, this cosmic taunt
of solar fallibility is as inevitable
as it is occasional — so many

elliptical orbits, planetary rotations
and axial tilts – paths are bound
to cross and cross again. Of course we can't
watch. Like any decent myth of deity,
to look straight on is to go blind.
And it will come around again, bodies
lining up like they do. Even if I can't see
it coming. Even if I forget
that once I didn't know the danger
and I watched.

4.   Four years since my pulse built speed
at the sight of every gray and rusting pick-up
truck, since I've been fucked
by a man who told me to shut
up, since I fought him
with a snow shovel and a broken
foot until he threw down
the house keys and drove off.
Four years and the other coast. I do not think
of him ever. I am not
loving him now, misplaced in a swarm
of faces, searching each one
for the familiar, for any absurd chance.

5.   There isn't much left with Patrick
gone missing but a street booth plate
of *pad thai* and finding the right
bus home. Home, there's not much
else but the usual route down Cabrillo
to the grocery store, past
Joe's Liquor and the Happy Immortal
restaurant. I've never eaten
there. The pressure is too much.
Some things are meant
to last and I do my best to orchestrate
circumstance, clear a path. Some things just last.

And Patrick calls later, drunk
and mad, saying it's so like us to lose
ourselves. "We bought rings together.
Then you were gone."

San Francisco: Outer Richmond

She's speaking in tongues
    in cityscape of indefatigable fog
        and a street lamp defying *this is your sleep*
    in yesterday's drunk on the 31 bus
        bold with his bottle, generous
    in unending sibilance of pneumatic breaks
    in rooftops and chimneys and some threat of rain

    she speaks
spellbound in *patois* of someplace else
    finally, forced
    like hills that rise to fall
        and nothing reached for the climb
        and shackled to it
        like Sisyphus
        like electric bus to electric cable
        like fable of promiseland, inert, enduring
    go west young man
    stop short of ocean

        "candied ginger, Mission, *phở*
        burn off and through and dunes, dim
        and sum of what do you call this flower,
        this park. Rentiro. No, that's Spain
        and I can't claim a single tone in Mandarin
        a single term in tectonics. Anything
        but sourdough, anything but avocado.
        Look at me ache on these slant streets
        this stranger, this sleep,
        this so much crooked and limp"

    lips slipping on the spit of it
    the French kiss of it
    the other tongue

Precita Park, April 22

For once it's warm enough to uncover skin and I do
normal things. Like this. A festival. Two buses
and dozens of walked blocks to get here, but
it was either this or laundry. Wash the kitchen floor.
We all make choices and the ad said Earth Day. Free.
Come.

Eleven months ago you said come to San Francisco.
I said no without reason other than it made no sense
to haul my bedroom set 3,000 miles, and so. Here.
Precita Park in the Miss on's heart and only four porta-
johns for a crowd of thousands. Most drinking
beer. We all make choices and I could shed
my sweater, shoes. Uncover skin. I always
complain about the cold but you love this city.

A rock icon takes the stage to back a sit-com
star preaching bio-fuel, woodless paper, travel
mugs and I want to call my mom. My parents share
Earth Day with their anniversary, not by choice, by
chance. And so by chance I confuse ecology
with devotion and act accordingly. Compost food
scraps. Reuse plastic sandwich bags. I never planned
to stay past the year.

An eco-singer asks us all to touch the earth and I do,
thinking somewhere, sometime today you'll touch
it, too, but for now I'm part of something larger
than self-inflicted circumstance: sequestered
redwoods, Leonard Peltier and medical
marijuana. B.E. Smith walked point
in Vietnam and today he's walking point in the drug
war. Served time for self-medicating post-traumatic
stress. We all make sacrifices for something larger
than ourselves, or should. and see, I'm learning

something. You said come, never love, and we all
make choices. Turn away when we should. It's warm
enough today and I'm forgiving you for leaving.

The microphone cuts out and celebrities are jumping
up and down in the crowd for attention. In
San Francisco nothing seems odd except, for once,
I'm warm, thinking of devotion when I should be
thinking pesticides, buying products made from hemp.
Be a little more supportive.

Today is Earth Day and I'm barefoot in Precita
Park, forgiving. Yesterday, walking home from
market, loaded down with cageless eggs and local
milk, I turned onto our block. Twilight caught
the windows of every house and transformed
the street to strange, unfamiliar. For a moment, I
thought I had it wrong. Thought I turned too early.
Or too late.

Leaving San Francisco

It's a scene no matter where you go.
An odd cartography, this in-the-know and shifting
    boundaries, a measure of green in your wallet,
    his wallet.

    You don't know what a mojito is?
    Christ, it's only like the new
    Cosmopolitan. You can't escape it,
    like all this damn ahi tartar.

A map for nomads, fumbling between where you were
    and what in the world you were wearing.
Charted in slippery ink. Silk stitching.

My last night and we're blowing it out big:
    the Redwood Room at the Clift and I licked
    money to cloak my breath.
It's necessary, camouflaging this upstate New York moll
    who once went glam in a garage sale Marilyn Monroe
    wig, plastic silver sandals and a ten dollar dress.

    That shit don't go over in Union
    Square, babe. This isn't the Mission
    and you don't fit in with all those
    freaks and Mexicans, anyway. And
    who'll do your hair when you leave?
    You found God when you found
    Brenda at Mes Ami.

The cut, the weaving of neutrals and lowlights, a semi-
    perm on the midtones and I was saved.
I've got twenty dollar lip gloss just in case I'm caught
    in the same cha-cha black suede strappies I wore
    to the opera last week.

I don't mind this map of corseting, the lines tightening
    around each exhale, smudging as they shrink.
But I can't down the drinks, and the Redwood Room begs
    a distorted way of seeing.
It's not enough to say the teeth-bleached, glitter-blazed
    bodies crush everyone flat, deprived of topography,
    the legend gone missing and I can't find the "X"
    marked here, dig here for riches, come unbury me.

And this is no clue:
    a surfeit of gems and no place left to put them.

    What about him, the one with
    diamonds on his loafers? I'll buy
    you a drink if you kiss his neck
    without a word and walk away.

Sufficient: marking territory.

No atlas would reveal I don't belong, my scent alone
    betraying fraud.
My mother grew up in the ghettos of Hungary,
    pissed on her hands before she slept to keep them
    soft. Her legacy: a stink of recrement. Defeated grace.

    Call me, okay? I'll fly you to L.A.
    and take you to this little place
    that serves the best mojitos.

I pull a map of late-night bus routes from my purse,
    pretend to read until a fold of green unslips
    and a twenty is an easy chivalry.
It's enough to keep me going in any direction.
My hands are soft and taxis stop for me.
Every time they drop me off I'm almost home.

Chaos Theory of Travel Advice

A butterfly twitches in China

    nothing, really
    a shift measured six places to the decimal point's left
The atmosphere's perilous enough without her reckless flutter
    and there's no telling the weather in Wichita
Watch how the prairie grass lists in the absence
    of breeze, like a wall falling over

Funny, how chaos was finally tamed by a meteorologist
Sky inside computer code
    a program finding patterns that never settle
    down, defy mapping
Some things beg to be left alone

And it's funny, how I resort to reading stars for prediction
A cyclic shift of Cassiopeia and a celestial directive
    hovered above my west coast porch for weeks
Simply a matter of tricking gaze away from infinite
    coastline, trading bare feet for science, looking up
Six months in any direction and the constellation
    would have urged a different fate:
    Mesa, Modesto, Miami, Minneapolis

Initial conditions spin a long-term system to riot
Stars are dying through light years for a pinprick
    of luminescence
The earth's orbit wears a rutted path
The sky was clear and some things
    I don't leave to chance: Wichita

Some paths are straight enough to beg a forecast
Prairie grass drifts like ocean
But a butterfly is no tide
    her fluttered wings, no end

Eating Raw Fish in Wichita

Donna won't unfold her hands
    until the main course comes
And Ray's smearing maki with wasabi
    like it's peanut butter
Jane doesn't eat in front of people
And Bill's peeling fried pork
    off a stick
I keep stealing mints and passing
    them around the table
    miss my mouth when I pop
    soybeans from their pods

We're all ears and serious
    as stories bounce
from Jane's ex-husband's house
    fortressed with surveillance and attack dogs
    a car trunk full of guns
to the night Ray stopped an orgy
    at the famous but now defunct Sutro Bathhouse
There's no moral
    except that Donna bought earrings that she thinks
    are fun, and Jane won't tell us how many bones
    got broke
Ray was all coked up the night he made
    a mass of rutting bodies pause
    and listen to his jokes
And Jane still lets him wander naked at the pagan festival
He owns houses and Donna sells drugs,
    legitimately
Bill only gets a word in when silence flares
    like hibachi flame
But he's a philosopher and so

A chef is tossing bits of shrimp from his spatula
    to the eager, open mouths of patrons and he's missing,
    shellfish bouncing off of cheeks and chins to the floor
    but we're not watching
Donna folds her hands
I'm spilling smelt roe
    and it's important
    how we found each other
    why we stay

The Commute

Spanning the Arkansas River from Old
Town to Delano is a very naughty
bridge. Animals are not always treated
with deference in Kansas, but on
the bridge they loiter and spray, nip and sniff
unreproached. Domestics mix with strays. People
avert their gaze as if accidentally
witnessing the indiscretions
of a semi-royal family, vicious
when provoked. The naughty bridge does nothing
to control traffic, having bucked yellow
lines and road signs in the forties. Autos
are left to fend for themselves, windows rolled
down at their own risk, risking a safari
jubilant and unchecked, gulls leaving
footprints in fresh wax jobs, cats sidling
along tires, insurgent cyclists
picnicking on the asphalt without
helmets, throwing rich, store-bought morsels
to chipmunks and mutts. The air above
the bridge smells like baked apples. The water
slows irresponsibly beneath. Even good
Christians pause to stroke
a railing when they pass, saying, "This bridge
isn't so naughty. It just lives in difficult
times, doing what it must to get by."

Nobody leaves the station

Activity involving height and motion
     also involves risk.
          – gym mat caution sticker

And if we know the limits of our bodies and elemental physics?
There is still barometric pressure to contend with.
Undiagnosed allergies, interior wood-rot, diseased birds.
Man (*A*) sees Woman (*B*) across a crowded parking lot.
Early September weekday. Central Kansas.
He's late for work, lonely and regretting a skimpy, empty-calorie lunch.
She's blonde and frowning, but her sandals are strappy,
complicated with buckles.
The elementary school up the block is overcrowded and the Parents Committee
tore the jungle gym down overnight. A liability.
The store bought new mini-carts, perfect for shoppers who live alone.
None, however, are available.
Seconds tick and *A*'s caloric load diminishes by one. He thinks
of *B*'s difficulty with walking, her limited steps, calculations.
Sometimes he's out of breath after sex.
No breeze and nothing rises but heat from the pavement.
A Lexus backs out of a spot.
A thinks, "If it were Tuesday—"
thinks "Depending on pace and angle of approach, we
could meet at the electric door."
School lets out early for the lack of air-conditioning
and children are fearless, almost unbreakable.
Some are scraped, but quick.
The Lexus has a V8 engine and a driver who is thrilled
with acceleration.
B is halfway to the entrance, strides unpredictably deft.
A moves away from his car.

Petit Mal

I don't believe much in luck unless it's bad and self-generated
Cameron has a horseshoe cut into his head, like an ox-bow
     river carving a path around cowlicks
I learned a lot about topography in 9th grade, and I can guess
     small sections of the earth's fate from a low-flying airplane
In 9th grade I laughed – What do you do when an epileptic falls
     in a swimming pool? Throw in a load of laundry

Seizure boy, surgery boy, retard
Cameron knows the names and feels he earned them
The box in his chest sends a shock to his brain every 13 minutes
Seizures used to be a sign of witchcraft, but now I swipe
     a card across his heart to charge him up
Magnetics, I suppose, or benediction
The shocks make him thirsty
Meds make him quiet, enough tranquilizers to down
     a small poker club
I used to gamble but I had no luck with cards

He's twelve and rides the short bus, has trouble
     expressing complex emotions
Autism can arrest communication skills
Sympathetic acquaintances say he was dealt a bad hand
Cameron traces his hand again and again until I run
     out of paper
You are here, I tell him. I am here, too
He can spell a few names, writes them down and carries
     them with him
The smallest seizures carry him away for a minute or two
He comes back like a lecturing professor who lost
     his thought mid-sentence
I'm sad to be poor and living in Kansas
Cameron is learning to write my name

Gravel Language

Not all rocks. Sharp-edged
flats of shale that skid
across still water are notorious
for their one unintelligible syllable
as they sink. Boulders, too,
are mostly mute: resigned
to landscape instead of song, their glorious
vibratos hardened and choked.
And while cliffs and promontories, scarps
and reefs won't shut up, calling
like swallows across vast spaces, enraptured
with echo and wave, their language
is a privileged one, coded and closer
to God.

See that child squatting
the curb in front of the small brick house,
her jeans muddied red to the knees
in Georgia clay? She's speaking
with the gravel. She's in such deep
communion with the gravel she doesn't hear
her mama call from the front door.

The gravel says, "refugee."
The child answers, "yes."
The gravel begs, "rescue us."
The child shoves fistfuls in her pockets,
not doubting the seams will hold.
She never misunderstands the gravel. She
doesn't understand her mama's exasperation
at the door or at the hamper.
Gravel has been through so much, she thinks.
I can't be its only friend.

This Place

This is the room with a view of the el, and beyond
    it the river, the brightly-lit buildings of mid-town, the suspended
    arcs of the Triborough Bridge
This is the view marred by the panicked flight of the shadow-sparrow,
    a spasm haunting its wing
This is the chair where the faithful sit, watching the bird fly back
    and forth above the alley, stranded above
    the dunes the blizzard left
This is the blizzard that travels south-southwest, turning
    to rain when a hunter puts down his bag of rabbits and kneels
    at the edge of a lake

Winter will soon end for all of them – the faithful, the hunter,
    the bird, this place
This place that winter makes
    that makes the city more imagined than the hunter, that
    makes the faithful mourn the bird before it ends
    its flight

Tracing the Distance

So the spirit tries for another life,
Another way and place in which to continue
      —Theodore Roethke, *Meditations of an Old
      Woman*, "First Meditation"

A Body in Motion

The body's weight is not unbearable
Bones, skin, muscle, blood, the precious churning
    alchemy of kidneys and liver – no burden
The starver's celebration of restraint – irrational
Guilt is no cousin of ingestion
When you fly, would you rather crash
    into land or water while you gut-panic
    the turbulence?
It's a commitment – crashing, digestion

Bodies have hollow spaces and I'm no
    container, not even for brine and its crapulence
I'm a failure at vomiting
Half a fist down my throat and nothing
But to crash on land, that's a different sort
    of nothing, a floating up and ash

It's indelicate to speak of bowels, a slowed process
    threatened by every maverick variable: menstruation,
    clams, winter, extra calcium
Unjust, the alien orange or walnut or whatever
    using my body like some gestational pod, roosting

I am not guilty of eating
    just a little disappointed with what's necessary
When animals are threatened, they evacuate
    their bowels for swifter flight
A crash can happen at any moment, no warning,
    no telling which topography has turned
    to mouth underneath

The Scurvy

Even disasters are mercenary
and you're giddy
    coming from the East
    paying for road
An earlier spring at each mile marker bears witness: nobody
    suffers like you

You speed toward the reach of the toll booth attendant
He'll wait on that 35 cents while you speak your autistic ministry
    of interstate 80
No telling how much tragedy he's clocked
    smoking and sliding coins across exhaust until there's nothing
    left in his glassed-in box but the listening

This is what costs: you saying
    she's so lovely
    she makes you just want
    and what she swallows
    satellites
    citrus
    the pulp and the peel
    she sways regardless
    lunatic arms and I take pills for anchor
    for the authority of something else
    but she's diseased
    some deficiency, some pox
    her bones are loose and I left right after she bit and found
    the first tooth embedded in my chest
    it looked like a pill and I swallowed

But you're no seventh son
no vision, no addictions
nothing but the toll guy's glance, his exhale
nothing but a mid-sized sedan holding up traffic
and so nothing
you pay your toll
you drive on

Split

I have an ocean and you have an ocean
and so it was not chance, that we would meet,
become lovers. Just a careless stroll along
a footpath etched into earth through nine states.
Simple as walking, my ribcage, your porch swing,
that age-old story of small towns, small love.
Tonight I watched the Pacific waves break
and recede, dragging grains of coastline under.
I know the Atlantic is as hungry to shrink
the distance between coasts as her beloved,
hungry to meet and mix in each other's salt,
marooned without feet to cross their ocean,
this land so thin no love is accident, no
meeting chance, no distance a mistake.

Landscaping

Ex-boyfriends appear like daffodils
after a slow and stuttering melt. Last
autumn squirrels dug up bulbs, ran off
and buried them in places you'd never
expect to find a fragile toast of spring.

I've forgiven myself for not being much
of a gardener, resenting the maintenance
of dirt, but when I spot errant blooms by
the yield sign at the curb or beneath the dying
oak that, I swear, this season I will put out
of its misery, I admit, this is not what I
intended.

       You'd think I wouldn't be wounded,
thirty one and not all that good at monogamy,
crossing paths with the ones who strayed.
Greg, outside of Philly, looking like Clint Eastwood
seven years after the final scene. Mark,
in my doorway, asking for a place to crash
on his way to the city where he left me.

               It's
hard not to confuse my affection for them now
with my desperate, perfected love for who I was
then. Hard, not to want to dig beneath roots,
lift them up, claim them. The daffodil beneath
the oak is ridiculous. I have a space. The earth
has softened.

Pulled over and, ashamed, I tell everything

"It is a small city, sir
       and I keep my least favorite lipstick in my coat pocket just in case
My stomach twists itself around my ribs to force the truth and that's why
       I seem shaky, maybe suspicious, but if you'd just listen
My favorite is a thick merlot that clings to the edges of my lips and turns
       my skin, my eyes Mediterranean
If I was wearing it now you'd understand how I wasted it staining
       his windshield with obscenities
He tells me lies, limp ones with frayed ends
I know every pick-up truck in this damn town, but location
       is more revealing at 4 am than during the daylight
       which lends itself easily to explanation
This is becoming habit
Don't write that down, I have a day job
I'm just telling you these predawn aching roads love me now but turn
       ugly when I face them in the morning
I do not wander aimlessly
I know which windows should not be illuminated, the one-way streets
       dissecting logic, my lover's caution
I make up stories, worse than truth I'm sure, but necessary
       to rationalize this talk-show caricature I've become
       and I would not call this stalking

He says he loves me
       spreads his hands across the small of my back to hold
       the arch, to measure my rising, my greed
Motive and extenuating circumstances compliment each other nicely
       to justify a criminal act and so do not apply to me
I don't cause scenes and this cheap shade of Toasted Almond is my only
       arsenal and all I can do is accuse
It does not last long on lips but brands glass and chrome with a slick
       smear that limits vision and won't wear off
He locks his truck doors now
Don't write this down

He left my home tonight in a shirt I bought him, the blue he didn't like
    so I returned it for brown
I disappear in brown and he is hopeful but not so fortunate
You're not the only one to tell me to go home and, angry, he also speaks,
    in shallow breath, of faith
And I ask you, am I not a strong woman?"

Caution

I'll show you once
    a sample, a beware
    a double dog dare for too much man and I swear
    I won't call you sissy if you can't take it
You rushed the field once without a helmet
    concussed and legs buckling
    but that was college ball and you were benched
You've no coach now to call you back

And so this
    a warning, a shoulder, a camisole strap
The warning
    a mercy, a boast:

I will crumple your half-assed romance
    like cellophane wrapped around an empty
    pack of cigarettes
I will break your music
    your code of distress
I will take you apart
    no simple dismemberment
    some taste of rusting muscle

I will lose you, piecemeal, in my back pocket
    crowded with bus tickets, sketched maps,
    and other bits of tinder for the pyre
I grow limber, sweet and hissing, in the fire

I will pull your pieces in

Lessons in Stalking

1. Assume a common scent, something harmless: bread, baby powder, salt fish.

2. Following is a poor synonym and hysterical. Leave it to the stupidly obsessed and broken-hearted. [1]
    A. Anticipate is not enough. Predict.
    B. Oracles are mischievous and unfaithful. Become your own. Just one more skill to master, similar to grammar, based on math and breath. Memorize this:
        i. algebraic formulas
        ii. geometric theorems
        iii. doumbek rhythms
        iv. the properties of magnetism
        v. the gravity of myth
        Their functions are clear and don't merit explanation. [2]

3. Caveat: This is not a charted series of locations. This is not some coded spy-game pubescent, outgrown. This is not about getting close or being loved. This is not without impact, not without sin. This is atrophying muscle to fit inside a habit, a skin.

4. No contact. [3]

5. Disguise is conspicuous. Blend in.

---

1. This doesn't mean you shouldn't practice different strides until stagger is as casual as stroll.
2. Explanations of functions:
    i. the logic of hours and distance remaining.
    ii. the best angles of interception, the room for error, the principles of parallel lines
    iii. the unconscious is ritual of personal chaos. It has its own timing and conquering instance when it assumes the privilege of truth.
    iv. bodies are magnetic (proof: the iron smell of blood). Magnets attract, repel.
    v. the self-fulfilling prophecy of subject, of stalked.
3. If contact has already occurred: Contact is a breach in protocol I can't help mend. No situation is ideal or solid textbook but there's no quick fix when anonymity lacks. Things get ugly, violent.

6. Amass the necessary objects:
    lip balm, pedometer, stop watch,
    quarters, compass, sidewalk chalk,
    wire cutter, glass cutter, box cutter,[4] bus map, flask,
    cell phone, salt lick, trail mix, plastic bags,
    leash, vendor's license, tchotchke merchandise[5]

7. Subtle cues betray eccentric for insane, comical for dangerous, nuisance
    for disturbed. Interaction with authorities is inevitable. Assume the identity
    of the easily dismissed.

8. Learn the woman's role of ballroom dance.

9. Stalking is reclusive and shares no intimacies.[6] The perimeter or ritual
    claimed by stalker and owned by stalked doesn't count and confirms: you are a solitary
    thing. Lonely. This distance is the closest that you'll get and it is, at best,
    empirical.

10. The final lesson finds the ending – frostbite, chapped lips, the itch of stagnant
    muscles, scraps of notes. You understand now? Preserved. The oil from your
    finger alters the precision of a dart's metal tip, will cause a halogen lamp
    to explode.

---

4. Occasional instances of buildings, barriers, fences – arbitrary obstacles that can't be
   sidestepped, and a little bit of criminal commitment casts out the last chance cowardice of
   turning back.
5. Two suggested reasons for repeated presence on a staked-out sidewalk corner: lost dog,
   hawking wares.
6. Intimacies:
   a) the biblical know.
   b) familial and its substitutes.
   c) legal institutions and verisimilitudes.
   d) most versions of friendship including those based on mutual addictions.

Seeing my neighbor naked in his kitchen

I thought all intimacies were best left to necessity
or chance. Yesterday he sliced his thumb attempting
to replace my windshield wiper. He broke it, instead,
and bled on my hood. And it's true my gaze
does tend to migrate to lit, uncurtained windows
with guiltless interest, honing my skills of immediate
and uncanny deduction. That's not peeping.
That's personal development, discarding options.
And I never thought it would be so hard, putting on
a new wiper. The old one came off with a twist
and a tug. But some mechanics aren't simple,
and some instructional materials mock.

It was accidental, of course. My bedroom window
facing his kitchen, my habit of waiting too late
to pull the blinds. I struggled with it for fifty minutes
before he came out, playing the cool kid
in high school shop. Or maybe it was intentional,
his timing, his pose without gesture beneath the overhead
light, a pelvis like coastal plain.

He was embarrassed, resorting to force
when the rain came. That's how he broke
my windshield wiper. That's how he cut his thumb.
And he was vulnerable. No. Vulgar. Ringlets
of pubic hair, plump cock, picking at the band aid I put on
myself. The auto parts clerk took back the pieces
without asking, walked me to my car and showed me how.
He could see everything. Some parts are simple
attachments. I closed the blinds and he watched.

The Butter, the Bottle, the Sugar Bowl

Some things melt when not kept
properly – chocolate, lipstick, a halo.
He slouches in the kitchen, shirt sleeves rolled
to the elbow, a stick of butter warming in
his hand. (She smiled once, to find him
        like that, her dress wrinkled from the drive
        to get the good bread, her mouth slicked
        magenta, her giggle - a halo.) Already,
the wine is opened, his mouth a sponge, the bottle
spilling, the butter - a thorn.

She is in his city
somewhere. (She never waited for dessert, ruined
        her mouth with chocolate before the bread.
        If there was no chocolate, she'd dip her finger in
        the sugar bowl, her mouth - a halo, her giggle -
        a scratch.) He unwraps the butter, grabs
the bread, wonders what the grain feels before the cutting,
before the butter thins, melts into and below.

Cure

If he confessed an addiction to honey?
Suspected a nutritional deficiency that sent him straight
      to the chocolate-covered combs and paraffin shakes?
Fondled beeswax candles in the upscale gift store
      until the sales clerk suggested a purchase
      was the only honorable gesture remaining?
You've seen the empty jars littering his counters,
      tasted a lingering sweetness each time you kissed
      his fingertips.
He has a stable job and an affordable mortgage, stylish
      shoes and a well-kept aquarium of temperamental
      tropical fish.
What animal doesn't shed its skin?
Submerge him in water to assist.
The process is itchy but edifying.
Underneath he gleams and quivers.
What he wants is what he always wanted,
      but in a new, beautiful way.

Ode to My New Food Processor

In my twenties, I chopped.
I crushed vanilla wafers, one at a time, by hand.
I hammered nuts.
Once, in desperation, I threw them in the coffee grinder.
That was a mistake.
Appliances are commitments. Like pets.
I found you in a home improvement store next to the blenders.
On or off or pulse.
That got me. Pulse.
My boyfriend talked about combining kitchens when I put you in the cart.
The instruction manual is unimaginative. Really limits your potential.
I won't make cheesecake ever again.
It's like a forced march.
But, boy, what you do to cooked kale and old potatoes.
I saved the warranty but didn't mail in the little card.
Not sure how the administrative stuff works anyway.
And, anyway, you're not breaking down.
Not even when I force feed you frozen cheese.
I'm talking about economy. Efficiency.
He thinks we should move in together by the end of summer.
My knives were growing dull and I don't own a sharpener.
You've replaced things I never had – a potato masher,
a cheese grater, a lemon reamer.
I'm lying about the lemon reamer.
That's something to register for when wedding
guests are habitual shoppers at Williams & Sonoma.
Still, you don't crush ice and I resent that a little.
I like my countertops uncluttered but now I'm thinking about a blender.
He has a toaster, a cake pan, dessert plates, a cooling rack.
My brother told me that I'm not the marrying kind, but my brother
doesn't eat a lot of vegetables.
Add it all up and I've probably spent a solid month chopping vegetables.
You slice through daikon root in less than a second.
Is it wrong to find that thrilling?
It's not that time is running out.
I don't mean to put this all on you.
I mean, I'm sorry the coffee grinder broke.
I mean I'm thinking.

Decline of the Blue Plate Special

They owned it most when they didn't
belong, waiting like mental patients against
the door, headlights smacking their eyes
in passing. The wait staff still
didn't know their names and they didn't
notice. He always paid and she always
wiped the rim of the ketchup bottle, hating to leave
evidence of appetite. They sat,
staring out windows polluted
with breath, he thinking he could do better, she
thinking she could do better, neither believing
this Union Street diner, its tic of blue
neon scabbing the sky, blinking
Diner blinking Open blinking Diner
blinking Open, could last another month,
gimping each hour away with low rent
biscuits and bacon grease. But it goes.
It lasts. It goes on forever.

Strategy of a Kiss

Begin at hinge, not lipped. Lidded. Outer canthus.

Ascend to eyebrow. A gentle press. Dry.

Arc to lacrimal duct. Don't rush. Laparoscopic
tongue, blindly.

The nostril curve. Don't linger.

Earlobe like an artichoke leaf. Savor.

The jawlined jugular. Fingertips can place
the pulse, the heat. Rest your lips. Regress.

Revive for clavicle. Slide

                              to sternum. Trap
breath and wait for condensation.

Nipple can be tricked, cajoled. Take between
your lips and cast a mold, a certain fit,
a memory.

The inside of elbow to wrist.

Bite middle knuckles, suck each fingertip, exhale
across palm so breath skims over the edge like falls. Drag
lower lip like the forgotten barrel.

Change your angle. Shoulder blades and sharper tongue.
Exact perimeters.

A railway of vertebrae, the concave links. Ride syncopation,
pulsely.

Two shallow dimples at the small of back, the span
between—pastry. Give a little sugar, little glaze, a drizzle
down the side.

Waist requires geometry and focus. Estimate trajectory
of abdomen. Aim for navel. No puckering.

Pace the thigh but take no shortcuts to the ankle.
The calf is no Kansas highway. Horizon,
a field of sweet corn. Graze.

Skim the metatarsal fan like swallows on a wire.

Strand yourself at toes. Beached. Reach for the water
sweating rings on the nightstand.

Repeat it all, reversed.

Repeat.

Love Letter, False Starts

Sweetie pie, pumpkin pie, my Russian meringue. My missing
game of hangman. My leavening bread, my broth. My sinsemilla,
my sense of brick, my lack of it, my lack. The small of my back
and sore and rub. My pillowed skin, my raisins, golden, wrinkled
in sun. My cinnamon, my cardamom, my house of cards collapse.
My careful with knives. My Bluebeard's brides. My sonnet, my broken
up song, my deep South. My scholar, my thief and liar and braggart
and thief. My brief moments of welling, my swell, my tide, my scent
of honey dew. Honey. Do you want to be on top, my
sweet? My very sweet. My pie.

Mapping the Spaces Between

Yet for this we traveled
With hope, and not alone,
In the country of ourselves
  — Theodore Roethke, "The Harsh Country"

First Part: To the One

Saturday, March 6
Wichita, KS

After the airport, I walked
　　the perimeter of the park, thinking
　　life to be just this: some place else
and going, I drove toward a moon we thought
　　was full the night before
Tonight it proved our underestimation of things completed
and I then watched clowns in white-face mocking
　　human drive for conquest, reproduction
Once I did not love you
I don't know when I did but estimate phases
Today you left at 4 pm and beginning absence
　　is the hardest – no memory of coping, no progress

Sunday, March 7

Today I planned six phone calls, the laundry, the groceries, some
cleaning, some grading, slicing the ripe pineapple, salting
the soybeans, making a salad, the dressing, a two-mile run,
the last 108 pages of *The Long Fuse*, a 1965 study of the causes of WWI. I
thought about white-face, revision and this on page 256:
    "The Emperor was worried about his moral
    responsibility for 'thousands and thousands
    of men who will be sent to their deaths'
    (Russian casualties in the war were to be
    about ten million men, including some
    two million dead)."
How remote you seem, how sweet the fruit

Monday, March 8

Cambridge earned its name with bridges
By now, you've found some coffee shop of damp brick and clipped
    enunciations
Wichita sounds like feral cats sparring for downwind position
We're both academics, so I'm not jealous grading papers
    I should have graded when proctoring your class, my window
    open to animal noises
Already you have tomorrow
History isn't just time, it's what you leave behind
Your espresso will taste good and disappear quickly
I mark another page, here, in this hour, bridging my day, yours

Tuesday, March 9

I want to tell you about the climbing wall and muscle
    memory, how bad the boys were today, all fuck
    you energy and no attempt at civility – not worth
    the 20 bucks a day the father pays me
You think I am good but I'm not
This body, this pattern of pulses and contractions
    that got me vertical past the overhang, grabbed
    Corey and swung him to standing, almost slammed
    him into a wall
But to make my muscles forget is to make my muscles
    forget everything – the rough fingergrip of granite,
    the small corrections, the way I learn to lessen –
    how much you trust when you trust your body
    to mine

Wednesday, March 10

The blood came early, as if my body felt
    around when waking and found some thing missing, sent
    out a search party
You sent word today of wrinkled clothes, a cold
    that won't subside in time for the conference, a real city
I leave the ache unanesthetized, my muscles
    preoccupied with their business, unaware of three trains
    barricading 21st Street on the way home
But it's so pretty and earnest, seeping expectantly,
    not knowing this place not good enough, that you've gone
    too far away to be found

Thursday, March 11

I drank tonight, baby.
I tried to make connections, but I made bold,
    heavy-bellied miscalculations – craving
      the salt of the smoked almonds, the low-throated bulge
      of goat cheese, a Pepper Grove pinot noir
And you know how I forget stopping, tortilla chip after
    chip, not knowing what taste I'm missing, which part of my tongue
    feels deprived
The company was engrossing but they left me with a sharp
    provolone in the kitchen

and how many ways can I inflict without you
    to stop me
You did not write today
    did not anticipate my greedy greedy mouth, my filling up
    on what's available

Friday, March 12

and after all, it was only cheese, a few nuts, sticking
    a wet finger to the bottom of the bag for the grit
Still, I made corrections – my first bite of apple at 4 pm
My morning class, dance, practicing mime and expression: ecstasy,
    vanity, rage
I was good, anticipating shame, but that wasn't part of the exercise

And what is her name? Your colleague extending the kindness
    of her home and a week's company, an invitation
    to her invitation-only conference not quite in your field
Astounding, a woman like that still single

And, honey, I'm sure you're representing well,
    with your two new slim-fitting sixty-dollar shirts
    and a switch to a hip new pair of specs
Philosophers *respond* to cutting edge fashion
The grants and the job leads must be land-sliding down
    your richly-threaded back and O! all those offers
    of collaboration

My instructor was displeased with only one
"Show me you in love."
I gestured, surprised, there, to see you

Saturday, March 13

Chandra's 30th Birthday at the Shamrock

Parties prove my mediocrity
I'm tempted to tell you nothing but
    I bought new stockings and the evening ended
    at the Nifty Kitchen on South Broadway
Before that, I could have flown, but didn't
I didn't mind the ideological boy in the corner
    but the one who called me saucy disappeared
I romanticized Mafia links on the Italian side of the family,
    but really it was just on with the jacket and gone
and I tried telling Brian that Floyd was Floyd Skloot
    but no one believed my connections
Chandra can glide all night long – like the ground
    is a stepping stone shifting beneath her
In the end, I skidded in clumsy imitation, ate
    a side of biscuits no one envied

Now, a bird sings hours before the ink of early morning hints a dawn
Listen
You can pity the ambitious for trying too hard, burning their luck too soon
You write, "I miss you."
You write, "Tomorrow we leave for her cottage in the country."
The bird, gone silent, once more breaks its throat on song

Sunday, March 14

I have something to tell you.
I went to your place to water your plants and found the toilet running.
I fixed it, folded towels, washed a cup, picked away dead leaves.
Still, your water bill is going to be phenomenal.

Monday, March 15

Yes, my love, yes.
I miss you, too.

Tuesday, March 16

As if you took logic across the ocean,
    hold it in your lap like a pet
I pet its restless shadow, attempt to soothe its eastbound
    eager stretch and slow vanishing as the eleventh day ends
Today I taught the concepts of plot and tension, the rate
    of revelation and the space good writers leave
    vacant for questions
Combed students for certainties we all agreed
    on – *in medias res* – my lecture betraying
    the chalk-drawn arrows connecting conflicts, charting
    a good yarn
"The reader is caught," I said, "by what she apprehends,
    trusting you to revise her straight out of easy conclusion"
When I dismissed the class – the board a mess – all our falling
    actions were left unresolved

Wednesday, March 17

Orpheus sings, in Ovid's Book X, of inversion:
    daughter fucking father
    hosts eating guests
    lover accidentally killing the beloved
In seminar, we skim over the indelicate, focusing
    instead on Venus' unfortunate scrape
    with her son's laced arrow
She was ridiculous – hiking up her robes
    to run barefoot after some pretty mortal boy,
    joining his hunt
What I'm dancing around is this:
    I am a woman of solid analysis
You write, "Kate asked me to stay at her house for the rest of my time
    here. I'll commute to London and save a thousand pounds!"
I admit, I did not reveal the entire unfolding of Chandra's party – the one
    from the west coast, the mathematician – withheld information,
    I teach my class, from the imperfect point of view

Thursday, March 18

The West Side has its bastions:
    the cock crowing the mid-afternoon traffic speeding past its yard,
    packed-dirt roads connecting residential tracts to pavement, giving up
    dust with rutted shrugs
We have our Starbucks, our Subway, our Payless, our intersections
    of multiple turning lanes and timed lights
but the man crossing 25th on horseback is not the anachronism
Time has an inertia that makes sense
And how will you find Kansas when you come back?
Today the refinery burned, its soot-black breath billowing sky
The outlaw in me nods acceptance, inhales what she should
This is an imperfect place, spinning its days slow, taking what action
    it needs to take to accommodate the coming change
    and preservation

Friday, March 19

Shush. I'm only playing games of possibility, practicing
    dramatic tension, keeping myself entertained
    while you and Kate lock cultivated minds
As if milking a two-bit flirtation for a couple of days provides
    any distraction, all my marvelously witty quips prolonging: *no*
    and *no thanks* and *no thank you*
A va-va-va-voom cheek-peck to be polite, his wrist
    glancing my back as he leans into
    string theory, "filaments in various vibrational modes"

Tonight, three scotch and sodas at Kelly's and Chandra
    reminds me of my conscience – constant and glittery
    and slightly semaphoric is its "look at me, look at me"
    endless rant
As if the displaced Berkeley mathematician
    could wave his arms as wildly
As if he'd want to

Saturday, March 20

After waking, I walked
    the perimeter of the park, thinking
    life to be just, or even decisive
You write, "I'd like to see you in more skirts."
    and I hit a sale at Dillard's coincidentally
Crinoline's been resurrected and I've got
    a pair of red strappy sandals itching
    for debút
but the dressing room mirror is not your gaze
    nor someone else's
Clusters of cherries in the fabric's pattern, and I
    will paint my lips to match
The middle of absence is not easy to recognize,
    though the mirror stares back, saying, "You.
    You."

Sunday, March 21

After pacing the apartment, after addressing
    the pros and cons on paper, in ink, after
      making the call and the subsequent second guessing
I went to the park and I ran,
    wishing for runway, for cockpit, for distance
      greater than paltry-muscled legs and measured breath
And direction? Behaved
I could survive on broth and saltines with these intentions

He sat on my couch twitching as I unfolded a map, traced
    a span I hope to travel, but not yet
He said, "I'm a patient man."
And me? My endurance flags, trying to outrun
    this foreign heavy heat that fuels my forward motion,
    that anchors me to ground

Monday, March 22

And you? At yesterday's protest in Trafalgar Square,
      rain-soaked and jostled by disgruntled socialists,
      you were the man I loved with good reason
Today I studied the lure of fascism between world
      wars, its fundamental promise of regenerated nations
      if they'd just get off their sissy parliamentary asses
      and effectively slaughter for the good of the state
It's crucial to construct a parallel between 1939, 2003,
      London, Wichita, a politically impeccable conscience
      and due respect
Instead, I place a pen between the pages, close
      my eyes and envision his body, mine

Second Part - To the Other

Tuesday, March 23
Lawrence, KS

In El Dorado, a tower burns
I could see it from Augusta, like the moon rising
    angry, its blazing horns catching the horizon,
    disintegrating its seam
To believe in omens is not enough
To interpret correctly is to have no need
    for omens at all: passion/Gomorrah
You said the terms are mine, the decision when to turn
    and in which direction
Now, I spread myself across the guest double bed
    in Em-and-Kevin's townhouse
They said the tower burns when the refinery's in trouble
They said the tower's always burning
They sleep down the hall, contented

Look, you
    with your patience and wayward equations, tangents sneaking
    from your fingertips like tapers
There's always fuel that begs ignition, a greedy flame that feeds
    on something other than itself, that harbors no false hope
    of anything rising from ash
And the one across the ocean – he is a good, good man

Wednesday, March 24
Chicago, IL

The plane fell into Chicago
That's what the flight attendant said over the loudspeaker
    and it's true
Those last couple inches were at gravity's insistence
    and so I can once again claim a lack of control over
    circumstances, put my faith in the bumpy ride
My fourth year at this conference and I'm becoming
    more efficient at self-deflation — only an hour of wandering
    the lobby to find a high school alumna smiling
    from a dust jacket, praised and widely published in all
    the right scenes
Already I've crossed paths with Tim and Jeff and Gerry and Erika,
    count their books aloud, introduce them by titles
And here, in the asylum of Au Bon Pain, I'm so rife with language
    the cashier corrects me when I call a rosemary bialy a thing,
    my fork and butter, stuff
I tell him,
    "I am the dark horse
    the poor gypsy swishing her skirts
    the slow burning ember
    the apple untasted, uncut"

Thursday, March 25

You call, and in our Midwest span of distance, you've become ridiculous
    – a strange desire's phantom poltergeisting my focus, throwing
    a tantrum now that it's been bested by a panel of confessional poets
I'm glad I'm gone, walking up and down Wabash beneath the el,
    its cornering screech cousin to my nerves remembering I once again   wanted
    to fuck and have so soon forgotten
To stay in Wichita is to stay in trouble and you have not yet won
Everyone asks about my love in England and I tell them
    "Tomorrow he comes home."
I let your voice go to message, leave it there, blinking
I heard poems today that made me cry and not out of envy
On the end-of-the-night dance floor I dance like something caged,
    then freed

Friday, March 26

And away, I breathe a wordless air
Fog swallows the skyscrapers' endings,
    and it seems this city has no boundaries
He hasn't been writing, he *understands* conference frenzy,
    the need for space, but I am lost
Waking up, hung over and worrying about dropping
    the pink invitation three times in front of one more
    literary idol, it's him I want, not you
This city begins at water, or completes itself there
I should know one end or the other, know that I am moving
    toward or further away
I haven't yet gone to the lake
Fog swallows it also, and him, and you

Saturday, March 27

I measure distance in guiltless footsteps, promenade
    the Magnificent Mile with Jeff, an old friend
    on whom an older crush has grown worn and giving
    like a well-used winter coat
When we reach the sands of Lake Michigan, I run
    the breaking waves barefooted, my ankles aching
    with rushing numbness
Like you and me, Jeff and I never kissed, never indulged in one
    illicit touch and we take photos of each other
    to catch ourselves
Today, my gesture of commitment was to finish all my lunch
Em said that every day she must choose to love
    or not to, no simple decision, no easy transition
    from dreams to waking to default
I wiped the bowl with my last piece of bread,
    stuffed it, dripping, in my mouth

Sunday, March 28

En route from Lawrence to Wichita

The tower in El Dorado isn't burning, though I started searching
    for its blaze as I passed Emporia's smouldering range, the managed   lines of
fire creeping alongside the interstate like a lazy battalion,
    the hills charred to a mirage of fertile loam
I don't understand the prairie, its need for forced beginning, but once
    I saved a lunar moth from extinction, waded the lake
    to skim it from the surface, let it rest on my palm as long as it needed
    to dry its flooded wings
There's a photo somewhere, capturing rapture,
    my connection to this creature that soon flew away
Some things begin by continuing
By continuing, some things turn to dust
I speed on to Wichita without stopping, anxious for homecoming
    because he is there
    and he is there
    and you
    and you

Coda

Here distance is familiar as a friend.
The feud we kept with space comes to an end.
— Theodore Roethke, "In Praise of Prairie"

Astronomy Lesson

Tomorrow I will rise at three,
drive north with you away
from the city lights' safekeeping
to watch the Leonid meteors
solder sky to galaxy.

But tonight I called my mom, and we talked
about turkey bones, estrogen replacement, weather.

She asked after you by name, a commitment
she stopped making after thirteen years of three-card
boyfriend monte. *This one could be it, I swear. This time
I am different*, and even the faithful catch on to being
conned, they just hang on

                          to one more round of shrinking
odds. Once, she pulled her veil from plastic wrapping,
draped it like a storm cloud and my neck still itches.

Tomorrow, when we rise at three,
drive to watch the fire arc
divides, leave behind pellucid streams,
the moon will be so full and high
only the brightest Leonids break
through, but we would never curse it.

You'll tell me how this works –
dust and ice orbiting
sun, reflecting – nothing more
than tiny grains, timing. I will think
how many, how fleeting, how distant.
Your arms elliptical around my waist,
I'll lose count.

I am grateful to the editors of the following magazines and journals in which the following poems first appeared:

5 AM – Eating Raw Fish in Wichita; Ode to My New Food Processor
Alimentum – The Butter, the Bottle, the Sugar Bowl
BigCityLit – Climbing Brian; This Place
DIAGRAM – Lessons in Stalking; Strategy of Kiss
Ellipsis – Outer Richmond; A Body in Motion
Harpur Palate – Gravel Language
Inkwell – Astronomy Lesson
Lake Effect – Ruby Skye
Mikrokosmos – Commitment; Decline of the Blue Plate Special, Leaving San Francisco;
          No Swimming
Nimrod – Precita Park, April 22
Pavement Saw – Nobody Leaves the Station; Seeing my neighbor naked in his kitchen
Rattle – Landscaping; Pulled over, and ashamed, I tell everything
SLAB – Your Bed
you are here: the journal of creative geography – Chaos Theory of Travel Advice
Willow Springs – Like a Sine Curve

Petit Mal appears in *Love You to Pieces: Creative Writers on Raising a Child With Special Needs*, Susan Kamata, ed., Beacon Press, 2008.

The poem "Mapping the Spaces Between" was original published in a slightly different version as a chapbook by Snark Publishing, O'Fallon, IL, 2004.

"Like a Sine Curve" received a 2005 AWP Intros Award.
"Commitment" received the 2005 Mikrokosmos Award in Poetry.
"No Swimming" received the 2006 Mikrokosmos Award in Poetry.

Special thanks to the New York State Senate for an Arts and Culture Grant, the New York Foundation for the Arts for a Special Opportunities Stipend, and the Jerome Foundation for a Travel and Study Grant. Thanks also to Albert Goldbarth, Jeanine Hathaway, and Ed Ochester for their encouragement and critical eyes. I am indebted to Theodore Roethke, whose wisdom guided me through this book, though I didn't know it until nearing the end. Finally, I thank my family and friends for their love and for lending me their stories and voices. I am blessed to share their landscapes.